Germaine Greer was born in Melbourne and educated in Australia and at Cambridge University. Her book, *The Female Eunuch* (1969), remains one of the most influential texts of the feminist movement. Greer has had a distinguished academic career in Britain and the United States. She makes regular appearances in print and other media as a broadcaster, journalist, columnist and reviewer. Since 2001 she has been involved in rehabilitating sixty hectares of subtropical rainforest in south-east Queensland; in 2011, she set up Friends of Gondwana Rainforest, a UK charity, to help in financing that and similar projects.

Little Books on Big Ideas

Germaine Greer *On Rape*

Fleur Anderson *On Sleep*

Don Watson *On Indignation*

Katharine Murphy *On Disruption*

Sarah Ferguson *On Mother*

Nikki Gemmell *On Quiet*

Blanche d'Alpuget *On Lust & Longing*

Leigh Sales *On Doubt*

Barrie Kosky *On Ecstasy*

David Malouf *On Experience*

Malcolm Knox *On Obsession*

Gay Bilson *On Digestion*

Anne Summers *On Luck*

Robert Dessaix *On Humbug*

Julian Burnside *On Privilege*

Elisabeth Wynhausen *On Resilience*

Susan Johnson *On Beauty*

Germaine Greer
On Rage

MELBOURNE
UNIVERSITY
PRESS

MELBOURNE UNIVERSITY PRESS
An imprint of Melbourne University Publishing Limited
Level 1, 715 Swanston Street, Carlton, Victoria 3053, Australia
mup-contact@unimelb.edu.au
www.mup.com.au

Text © Germaine Greer, 2008, 2018
This edition published 2018
Design and typography © Melbourne University Publishing Limited, 2008, 2018

This book is copyright. Apart from any use permitted under the *Copyright Act 1968* and subsequent amendments, no part may be reproduced, stored in a retrieval system or transmitted by any means or process whatsoever without the prior written permission of the publisher.

Every attempt has been made to locate the copyright holders for material quoted in this book. Any person or organisation that may have been overlooked or misattributed may contact the publisher.

Text design by Alice Graphics
Cover design by Nada Backovic
Author photograph by Neil Spence Photography
Typeset by Typeskill
Printed in Australia by McPherson's Printing Group

 A catalogue record for this book is available from the National Library of Australia

9780522874327 (paperback)
9780522874334 (ebook)

In memoriam Mum Shirl

On the afternoon of 13 February 2008, I twiddled the knob on my car radio and was startled to come across words spoken in a voice shredded with rage.

> The former minister mentioned woody weeds. I happen to represent an electorate that is suffering from what has been described as the greatest environmental holocaust in Australian history, the acacia prickly tree, which has now gobbled up six million hectares, almost an area the

size of Tasmania, in thirty years. All native flora and fauna have been destroyed by it. Who was the minister responsible for this issue and for doing nothing about the destruction of all this magnificent area, an area which is described on an old map of Queensland as being the richest natural grasslands in Australia? That pasture was utterly destroyed by the prickly acacia tree. Whose job was it to protect those grasslands and our native flora and fauna? It was this ex-minister. And he comes in here and has the hide to point the finger at the Labor Party for doing nothing about woody weeds! They have been here for ten minutes! It absolutely amazes me that a party that is trying to fight back into existence would put this man up front.[1]

The speaker might have wanted to roar, but his voice remained snagged in his throat, alternating between a snarl and a sob, sometimes quavering towards the hyena laugh of pure despair. The place was the House of Representatives. The occasion was the second reading of the Appropriation (Drought and Equine Assistance) Bills. The man speaking was Bob Katter, the honourable member for the Federal electorate of Kennedy, in rural north Queensland, a man with whom I would normally have no patience, but this time he commanded my attention, so real was his pain.

I know what it is like to be suffocating with rage. At my fiftieth birthday party, one of the guests, a relative of the host, decided to amuse himself by a little light mockery of us both for being concerned about the rights of indigenous peoples. Our tormentor was a television presenter from another country, cool, laid-back and witty. We shall call him Guy. What Guy said about aboriginal communities in his own country and in Australia was undeniable, but it was also callous, partial and cynically misleading. I began trying to explain why hunter-gatherer peoples had no interest in integrating with their oppressors or adopting the work ethic, but the ideas were too complex for dinner-table chat. As Guy entertained the company by caricaturing everything I said, I felt my heart rate increasing and my breath coming faster. The muscles of my throat began to ache and my mouth turned dry as ash. Then my voice went funny as if someone else was speaking through me. My eyes were stinging with unshed tears of scalding rage, but I wouldn't, couldn't give up until this smug bastard heard me out. He never did. The party broke up, the host spent the rest of the evening in tears and I went home, having eaten not one mouthful of my birthday supper. I shouldn't have let Guy rile me, should have kept my wig on, should have saved my breath to cool my porridge, whatever. But I couldn't. I could not have lived with myself if I had let him get away with the things he was saying. It was the very intensity of my indignation that squeezed my throat so tight that I couldn't talk properly. Now I was hearing the same grinding, gravelly, pain-wracked sound from Bob Katter.

Katter's was the voice of a man whose heart is hammering, whose veins are distended, who is literally breathless with passion. The man in his sights was Warren Truss, leader of the National Party. Truss had risen to express his support for bills originally brought to the House before the 2007 election when he was minister for Agriculture, Fisheries and Forestry in the Howard government. Katter was the next to speak to the bills but he never got around to it. He went for Truss instead. Truss was the man who, according to Katter, should have dealt with prickly acacia, an unfair charge if ever there was one. (Prickly acacia was introduced in the 1920s, and had its greatest growth spurts in the 1950s and 1970s.) Katter intoned a litany of examples of what he took to be Truss's negligence.

> He allowed the grapes in from California in the same month that one-tenth of the entire

grape production in California was wrecked by Pierce's disease … the pork case … black sigatoka … Spiralling whitefly … bluetongue disease … citrus canker … beef from Brazil, a foot-and-mouth diseased country … ended up on the Wagga Wagga dump, where pigs regularly eat …[2]

Like his father before him, Katter had for many years represented the interests of farmers of rural Queensland as a member of the Country Party, later renamed the National Party. For him and his ilk the effects of economic rationalisation and the decline of rural industry were catastrophic. Once the rural élite, farmers were going to the wall. Truss was now the new leader of the National Party from which Katter had resigned to contest the election of 2001 as an independent. Katter ranted on, probably to an all but empty house, with never a 'hear, hear'.

> If I speak with some passion and rage, it is because I represented nearly 300 dairy farmers; I now represent fewer than eight. Every single one of those people who exited the industry represent[s] heartache and bankruptcy ... Every four days in Australia, a dairy farmer commits suicide.[3]

Katter's was not an instinctual response. There was no immediate trigger that would have jolted his sympathetic nervous system into pumping out the stress hormones. The sensory input that animated him can have been no more than the bland sound of Truss droning on in his own praise and justification.

Could this have been sufficient to turn on Katter's limbic system so that the message was sent from the amygdala to the hypothalamus to activate the neurotransmitters which in turn stimulated the adrenal medullae to release adrenaline and noradrenaline into the bloodstream ready for fight or flight? Katter was never in danger from Truss. His anger was not engendered like the chemical reaction that activates animals to stand their ground or flee. It was the outcome of his critical judgment of how Truss had performed in office and therefore intellectual rather than physical in origin, and probably of long standing. Nevertheless it had immediate physiological effects. Every listener to the broadcast would have noticed the strange harshness of Katter's voice and the urgency of his delivery.

His blood pressure would have risen steeply as if he did indeed have a fight on his hands. Did he feel better after giving Truss what for? As the adrenaline ebbed, he probably felt let down and very tired, as if he had gone a couple of rounds in the ring. He may also have felt frustrated, because he didn't finish what he had to say. The speaker cut him off when his time ran out.

As I was to find out, Katter had reviled the 'cowards, idiots and lightweights' of the National Party many times since he had left it because it had 'rolled over and accepted the deregulation of the wool industry, the egg, the maize, the dairy, the sugar …' The representatives in the House that day probably thought 'Here he goes again' and went to the tea-room for the duration. Rage reiterated day in day out loses its charisma and becomes mere harping on one string. Impotent rage is bad for you; the action of rage chemicals puts acute stress on the heart and vital organs. We should probably not be surprised that in 2004 Katter, who was then fifty-nine, was found to be in need of a heart bypass operation. Nevertheless his supporters would want him to keep the fire in his belly, and he too must feel that he has a duty to the people he represents to keep his rage burning hot and bright, though it may kill him. In Shakespeare's play, when Hamlet is upbraiding himself for not killing Claudius, he wonders if he might not be 'pigeon-livered and lack gall to make oppression bitter'. A red-blooded man is not supposed to take insult and humiliation lying down. He should not let people get away with doing things he thinks wicked or unjust. He demands the right both to judge and to act upon his judgment.

> In speaking to this legislation today, and speaking with some considerable passion, it is my sad and sorry lot to represent dairy farmers ... if I speak with passion and try and hurt some of the people who have hurt us so dreadfully, then I am entitled to, just as the good Lord whacked into those money-changers in the temple ...[4]

Katter saw his passion that day as godly, and asserted his right to punish those who had hurt his people. To be effective, the natural energy in rage must be focused as a laser focuses light, so that it can slice through diseased tissue and expose corruption. The successful orator will mime rage rather than allow the real thing to overwhelm him. He will thunder, rather than gnash his teeth.

For almost seven years, from 1983 to 1989, Katter served in the Howard government, first as minister for Aboriginal and Islander Development, then as minister for Ethnic Affairs. As a man who says himself that he is 'not entirely white',[5] who grew up in Cloncurry where nearly half the population is of Aboriginal descent, he was much closer to the reality of life as experienced in Aboriginal communities than all but one or two of his fellow parliamentarians, yet he is said to have been absent from the House of Representatives when the bipartisan motion for an apology to the stolen generations was unanimously carried.

Suicide was not a new theme for Katter. In March 2005 it was he who rose to call the attention of the House to the fact that in the preceding three months in the Aboriginal community of Mornington Island, thirteen teenagers had attempted suicide; in the preceding nine months three had been successful; two weeks before, a fourteen year old had committed suicide.[6] In 2007, the small Aboriginal community of Fitzroy Crossing saw twenty-two suicides, twice as many as in the previous year, one of them an 11-year-old boy. Alcohol was involved in most of them; alcohol is probably involved in most suicides of dairy farmers. Katter would probably be surprised and displeased to find his suicidal farmers lumped in with self-destructive hunter-gatherers, but it is my contention that the force that drives suicide, for whitefella as for blackfella, is the same force that choked him in the House of Representatives that day: impotent rage.

Australian Aboriginal peoples have suffered far greater losses and outrages than Katter's farmers will ever be called upon to endure but most of them, if offered the opportunity to air their grievances for half an hour on national radio, would not take it. The rage that eats away at Aboriginal hearts is too deeply embedded to be trotted out and paraded in a talking-shop. Katter talked of banana farmers who had lost money from black sigatoka disease, of prawn farmers struggling against white spot, of the papaya fruit fly that took $75 million out of the industry, of the buy-out of Australian fishermen, of the tobacco farmers who were earning $200 000 a year. 'They were completely destroyed and got $150 000 in return!' he howled.[7] A man is not completely destroyed when he loses his livelihood, even if he doesn't get compensation, if he still has his health, his education, his family, his social network, his culture, his religion and his self-esteem. It was the suddenness of the farmers' fall from influence and affluence that so shocked Katter and his supporters; their trauma is recent and trivial, compared to the endlessly renewed catastrophe that white occupation has been for aboriginal peoples everywhere.

Most of the people who gathered on the lawns of Parliament House on that same day to hear the new Prime Minister Kevin Rudd say sorry for the stolen generations were white.

As the cameras scanned the crowd, looking for specially moving pictures, they found plenty of Aboriginal women of all ages, plenty of children, but no Aboriginal man who was not elderly. The object of Rudd's rhetorical exercise was twofold: one, he had to apologise and, two, the Aboriginal peoples had to be seen to accept his apology. There was never a suggestion that the Aboriginal peoples might jib. On news services all around the world, they would be seen to have been mollified. If Warren Truss had said sorry to Bob Katter for any part he might have played in the suicide of dairy farmers I doubt Katter's rage would have abated. Indeed, he might have been so incensed by the very notion a verbal apology would get Truss off the hook that he might have offered to punch his lights out.

Yet no one thought for a moment that the Aboriginal peoples would turn their backs on Rudd and his apology. Could it be that adult Aboriginal men did just that? The apology, meanwhile, was carefully worded so as not to leave the government liable for compensation. It fell out as Katter's friend Noel Pearson prophesied: 'Blackfellas will get the words. Whitefellas will keep the money'.[8]

Where were the Aboriginal men? Guy would have sneered that they were probably in prison. Certainly, many of them are in prison. On any one day 6 per cent of Australian Aboriginal men between the ages of twenty-five and thirty are in prison.[9] In any year a quarter of all Aboriginal men will be involved with the correctional services;[10] 22 per cent of the Australian prison population is Aboriginal;[11]

42 per cent of juveniles in the justice system are Aboriginal. In North Queensland 90 per cent of juveniles in custody are Aboriginal.[12] In 1995 there were twenty-one deaths of Aboriginal men in custody, one-and-a-half times the number reported for the previous year, and almost two-and-a-half times the number reported in 1992.[13] Though the trend has since been downward, in 2004, fourteen indigenous Australians died in custody.[14]

The poor are always more likely to be arrested, found guilty and given a custodial sentence than the affluent, but the frequency with which Aboriginal men find themselves in prison is not simply the effect of poverty. Flagrantly transgressive behaviour is a form of last-ditch resistance to alien authority. The person who is powerless, speechless and helpless has no outlet but to smash things and people. Rage prompts us to assault others and it is also the force that pushes us to lay violent hands upon ourselves. Anyone trying to understand what is happening to Aboriginal men, why it is that they drink themselves into insanity and death, why they rape and maim the people who love them, and why they so often throw their lives away, needs to understand the role played by rage. Rage cannot be easily disentangled from grief, but there is a gender angle too. Women do grief; men do rage.

> People are suffering grief on all accounts. Grief at losing a way of life, grief because they don't see a future, grief because you've just lost somebody. One of my friends is 22 and he's lost two friends in the time I've

known him. He's highly strung and he gets angry …[15]

A woman who expresses rage is a man-woman, a virago, because rage is masculine. Even in the vaunted British legal system and the systems descended from it, men have a right to rage, even to accumulate rage and hoard it till it reaches toxic levels. If a wife should displease a husband to such an extent that he loses control, his bottled-up rage pops its cork and he murders her, he can walk from the court scot-free. The barrister presenting the provocation defence will create a vision of the victim as having brought her fate upon herself, usually by nagging incessantly, giving the man no peace, and even mocking his sexual performance. Under English law a man who refuses to look for a job, lies around the house drinking and making a mess he will not clean up, and leaves his children unsupervised while his wife goes out to work to keep them, can kill his complaining wife and get away with it, provided he can prove blind rage. He will be deemed to have suffered enough, and she to have got what she deserved. Male rage is thereby privileged within the British legal system. In Britain a woman who killed her husband after enduring years of horrific abuse used to have no defence against the charge of murder, until the provocation defence was expanded to include such cases even though there was clear evidence of premeditation. The result was inconsistency and confusion. This was the wrong way to go.

In removing the provocation defence, Victoria and Tasmania have done the right thing. No one should be able to justify killing anyone on the ground that he or she was provoked. It makes no odds that in Victoria and Tasmania women will not be able to use the provocation defence. Every woman should understand that the proper thing to do with an abusive partner is not to kill him but to leave him, sooner rather than later. Law enforcement should be prepared to take her at her word, to provide adequate protection and to take up the case against her abusive partner. Having children by an angry man is not a reason to stay with him; it is in the interests of neither women nor children to remain in proximity to a man poisoned with rage. When unemployment rises, domestic violence also rises, which is a pretty fair indicator of how rage can be relied on to miss its mark and rebound on the innocent. Ineffectual railing does not reduce the quantum of rage, but adds yet another grievance to the already festering heap. Nowadays violent men are encouraged and sometimes sentenced to take courses in anger management, but to read the prospectuses of such courses is to wonder if the experts in self-control know anything about lethal rage and what it is like to live with it.

According to an American Psychological Association website:

> Anger can be caused by both external and internal events. You could be angry at a specific person (such as a co-worker or supervisor) or event (a traffic jam, a cancelled flight), or your anger could be caused

by worrying or brooding about your personal problems.

Airports are full of people who rant and rage uselessly about cancelled flights. Cars are full of people who snarl and curse at other drivers. To put such feeble bad temper in the frame with the rage of hunter-gatherer peoples is to have it dwindle to a pinpoint and disappear. Aboriginal rage is not of the order of road rage, or even of the rage of a nagged husband. It is not an excessive reaction to friction but the inevitable consequence of a series of devastating blows inflicted on a victim who is utterly powerless to resist. Any description of the action of rage in a hunter-gatherer society anywhere will provide a carbon copy of Aboriginal dysfunction.

In Canada in 1973, when it became obvious that in the course of eight years the Dryden paper mill had dumped more than nine tonnes of methyl mercury into the lakes and rivers which constituted both the resource base and the spiritual identity of the group of Ojibwa hunter-gatherers living on the Grassy Narrows Reserve 135 kilometres downstream, the government rounded them up and relocated them.

> Within a short period following relocation, sexual assault, child neglect and abuse, extreme alcohol abuse, petrol-sniffing and death through violence became epidemic within the community. Men beat women and abused children, women discarded dependent infants and abused children,

and older children beat and raped younger children.[16]

Sound familiar? After eight years of systemic mercury poisoning the Ojibwa were in no shape to deal with dislocation or, in the years that followed, to mount resistance to the clear-felling of their sacred forests, and the widespread use of herbicides.[17] Instead, they turned upon themselves and their children. The pattern is repeated with dispossessed hunter-gatherer peoples everywhere.

Such agonised self-destruction is the result of lifetimes of being pushed and dragged hither and yon, at every step losing more, and yet more, of what makes any human life worth living. Whole tribes have been wiped out; remnants of tribes have been forced to amalgamate with their traditional enemies; traditional lands have been alienated; people of disparate groups have been rounded up and resettled in polyglot assemblages in remote communities; others have been trucked back and forth from one dumping ground to another. Aboriginal peoples have lost all the important things Katter's farmers did not lose: their health, their education, their families, their social networks, their culture, their religion, their languages and their self-esteem. Australian Aboriginal peoples, desperate for healing of their many wounds, will struggle to return to their country, and once there will endure the most crushing hardship rather than come away again.[18] In Australia, successive governments have done their best to break the outstation movement, but they have not succeeded. Some of our highest-earning Aboriginal artists have chosen to live out their days in makeshift camps in the far wilderness rather than endure the manifold miseries of living in settlements like Papunya or Warmun. These are the lucky ones. For most Aboriginal peoples, return to a homeland is not an option; even for those who have returned, it is doubtful that their children will accept a life of such hardship.

Through all these vicissitudes the Aboriginal man has had no option but to succumb, in Katter's phrase, to 'roll over'. Every time he has become reconciled to yet another upheaval, he has had to endure yet another dislocation, yet another piece of draconian legislation, more and new state interference, as successive governments tinkered with solutions to the 'Aboriginal problem'.

> A not uncommon reaction in those who have been touched by violent death is to repress grief, guilt or anger until these powerful emotions can be released by the disinhibiting effects of alcohol. The feelings of aggression and rage normally suppressed in face-to-face encounters find expression during drinking parties which are the contexts for the beating, rape or other acts of violence that may lead to death.[19]

Some observers of extreme dysfunction in Aboriginal communities have blamed alcohol itself for the self-destructive behaviour that accompanies drinking. The call is raised again and again for access to alcohol to be limited, for take-away sales to be rationed, for in-house drinking to be curtailed, for only weak beer to be allowed, and for a total ban. All these arrangements have been tried. All that ensues is that the bootleggers, very few if any of them Aboriginal, make even bigger profits running grog into dry communities. Where the ban works, people are leaving for the cities where no ban can be brought in without invoking illegal forms of race discrimination. To enforce abstinence from alcohol is not to face the real cause of self-destructive behaviour. People without alcohol will make use of something else to provide the same disinhibition. The rest of us become silly and lachrymose or sleepy or amorous or querulous or sick when we have too much to drink. The man who becomes murderous or suicidal already has murder or suicide in his heart. Users of marijuana are usually pretty passive; in May 2006 Aboriginal users of marijuana in Wadeye in the Northern Territory waged war against each other, smashing houses and cars with axes and iron bars, hurling spears and boomerangs. Though the only way of obtaining surcease from violence may be to remove alcohol and other intoxicants from Aboriginal homelands, it will not be the answer. There may not be an answer.

The Aboriginal approach to drinking is itself problematic. The object of the exercise is not sociable tipsiness but disinhibition and oblivion. In Aboriginal peoples the suffocated feeling that is set free by alcohol is rage—howling, yelling, cursing, punching, kicking, murderous rage. In 1998, I stayed overnight at Arlparra Store on Utopia Station in the Northern Territory, where no alcohol is allowed. Around midnight I awoke to the sound of four-wheel-drive trucks pulling up outside the store; the bootleggers had arrived. An hour or so later all hell broke loose as the night silence erupted in shouting, screaming, and splintering of glass and timber. At the single women's camp in the morning, I found the senior law women stern-faced and silent. The other women told me in hushed voices that in the early hours drunken men had laid into the new health clinic with axes, and chopped it to bits. All the hard-won equipment that had just been installed had been destroyed. The senior law women were on their way to sit in judgment on the perpetrators. The men's rage was already at lethal levels; anything the women would do could only make the situation worse. The supreme pointlessness of the men's action at Arlparra is the best evidence that the black man's rage is directed not against the oppressor but against himself.

All kinds of prurience now bedevil any discussion of the true causes of the Aboriginal man's self-destructive behaviour, as if, in Marcia Langton's phrase, there is a corpse in the room that no one is allowed to mention. It is an issue so painful that I am almost afraid to bring it up, especially as Aboriginal people refuse to discuss it. Indeed, Langton has referred to any consideration of it as sexualising the issue, as if that meant reducing it to prurience and pornography. Nevertheless, at the risk of being accused of indulging in salaciousness for its own sake, I must point out the unspoken obvious: there would have been no stolen generations if the white man had kept his hands off Aboriginal women.

> Australians have yet to fully acknowledge how the widespread sexual use and abuse of indigenous women and girls literally spawned the stolen generations.[20]

Gillian Cowlishaw, now an Australian Research Council professorial fellow at the Sydney University of Technology, puts it more crudely:

> All the newcomers were men at first, which gave rise to the theory among Aborigines that the cattle, which the men so jealously guarded, took the place of their wives. In

fact the Aboriginal women did, and hence the brindle came into being.[21]

From the beginning of white contact in the 1780s, when the sealers abducted Tasmanian Aboriginal women, the white man has considered Aboriginal women his for the taking.

We were hunted from our ground, shot, poisoned, and had our daughters, sisters and wives taken from us . . .[22]

One version of events is that Aboriginal men willingly traded their women to white men:

The one great need the bachelor Europeans had on a frontier devoid of white women was the sexual and domestic service of Aboriginal women. The Aborigines quickly saw this as their best hope of gaining food, tobacco and alcohol in return. Aboriginal women offered themselves to the Europeans, or were offered by their husbands.[23]

It is hard to think of any society that would freely barter its women to an invader if it did not already find itself unable to survive any other way. The implication is that Aboriginal husbands were unlike others, and felt no resentment when forced to share their wives. Emeritus Professor Bob Tonkinson of the University of Western Australia did his research among the Mardu people at Jigalong, on the north-western edge of the Great Sandy Desert.

Aboriginal women relating their station experiences in 'the early days' often phrased their relationships with the pastoralists in terms of compassion and nurturance (both major cultural values): sorrow for the men's isolation from family and kin and compassion for their ignorance about the land. The dominant situation in the stations was one of accommodation and mutual benefit: pastoralism was unsustainable without Aboriginal labour, and once the Aboriginal people became sedentary, the intensifying needs for certain goods tied them ever more irrevocably to the frontier economy. From my observations in the mid-60s I concluded that as a result of their work in the homestead domain most women had enhanced their importance to both of the males in the frontier triad, thus laying part of the ground work for an increased assertiveness in their own society.[24]

By the time Tonkinson was studying the Mardu at Jigalong in the mid-1960s they had already suffered major disruption to their way of life. During the construction of the Canning Stock Route, Mardu men had been forced to point out the location of precious waterholes that once used by stock would have been lost to them and their people.[25] At night, to prevent their escape, the men were chained to trees. When an attempt was made to discipline Canning for this abuse, the judge decided that, as all the settlers in this semi-arid area resorted to similar tactics, Canning was guilty of no offence. The Mardu were at the mission at Jigalong only because they had been forcibly removed from their homelands, which had been chosen as the landing ground for Blue Streak missiles. Tonkinson was studying an already severely damaged polity. Once the Mardu had been forcibly sedentarised, they had lost everything that mattered to them. The goods they became reliant on were flour, sugar, tobacco—and alcohol.

There are two males in Tonkinson's 'frontier triad', the white one and the black one. White men have made huge fortunes in outback Australia, but their black co-husbands live in poverty. Some years ago I was travelling the Pilbara with a friend, a solicitor working for Rose Porteus, trying to find out if Lang Hancock had any heirs other than the litigious Gina Rinehart and my friend's client. I had heard, like everyone else, that when he was a young man Hancock had more than one Aboriginal wife. At an Aboriginal settlement near Wittenoom I asked if anyone knew any of Hancock's children. The answer came back that everyone did. I pointed out that Hancock's estate receives royalties on every tonne of iron ore that is shipped out of the Hamersley Range, and that his black heirs had a better right to it than Rinehart or Porteus. The man sitting next to me on the old iron bedstead looked down at his feet, pursed his lips and shook his head. The matter was not one that could be discussed by an Aboriginal person with a white person, or with a woman, and probably not with anyone. To date, only one Aboriginal woman, Hilda Kickett, has claimed Hancock as a father. In January 2003 John Rinehart, Hancock's grandson, agreed to release DNA for a paternity test, but though the test was flagged in the national press, it is not now clear that it was ever carried out. Rinehart made clear that even if Kickett was Hancock's daughter, she would have no claim upon his estate. There are children all over Australia who should have inherited from their white progenitors and have grown up in poverty and disadvantage instead. White Australia owes black Australia an immense fortune in unpaid child support, yet the payment of 'kid money' is one of the things that Australian racists complain about most vociferously.

Despite Tonkinson, there is evidence that the theft of Aboriginal women was resented, and that sometimes it was bloodily avenged.[26] Many of the women who ended up living in the white men's camps were children when they were grabbed; many of them were violently assaulted, held against their will, and even chained or manacled to stop their running away.[27] In 1900 at Ardock Station in Queensland, nine Aboriginal women were kept in a fenced compound for the use of the white station hands.[28] Women who succeeded in getting away would be hunted down, dragged back and thrashed within an inch of their lives. In one of the diaries he kept when working as a patrol officer for the Protector of Aborigines in the Northern Territory, TGH Strehlow reported how a station owner 'condoned his station-hands raping Aboriginal girls of eleven and twelve'. When the diary was mislaid, the person who found it showed it to the station owner, who complained to Strehlow's superior who took him to task:

Rape? Who said rape, Ted? Only you. What was probably said was that [the station owner] knew that his white station hands were having sexual relations with some Aboriginal girls. Nothing more. And that happens all the time. You know that … I don't call having a bit of nookie with an Aboriginal girl rape, Ted.

Strehlow replied:

I call taking a girl of eleven or twelve to bed rape. They're under the age of consent and they have been made to believe that it is obligatory on them to satisfy the white man's demands. In my view point that amounts to rape.[29]

Such practices prevailed on a massive scale across the whole continent, wherever the white man penetrated, in the words of Strehlow's superior, 'all the time'. Though we tend to think of the information now coming out about violence in Aboriginal communities as dealing principally with black-on-black violence, *Aboriginal Women Speak Out* reveals that in the Adelaide area the proportion of rapes of Aboriginal women committed by non-indigenous men is slightly higher than those committed by Aboriginal men.[30] In the earliest reports on Aboriginal health, children as young as twelve were reported to be suffering from syphilis.[31] In 1982 I picked up two runaway schoolgirls on the coast highway near Port Hedland in Western Australia; they had made their way down from Cape Leveque despite having not a penny between them. It would have been a rare truckie who would not have exacted his pound of flesh. In June 2004 Bakamumu Marika, an elder of the Aboriginal community at Yirrkala, presented the Northern Territory Police with a written report on the abuse of under-age Aboriginal girls by white men in Nhulunbuy, but no action was taken. The situation was referred to again in *Little Children Are Sacred*, the report of the Northern Territory Board of Enquiry into the protection of Aboriginal children from sexual abuse, but again no action was taken against the white perpetrators. Instead, in announcing the 'Intervention' the then prime minister John Howard managed to convey the impression that sexual abuse of Aboriginal children occurred solely within Aboriginal communities. When juvenile prostitution in Nhulunbuy finally made the headlines in April 2008, local magnate Galarrwuy Yunupingu stated 'Everybody here knows what is going on. It has been let go for a while and it should be about time that somebody in authority comes and stamps it out'. Mr Yunupingu, Gumatj elder, holder of the Order of Australia, 1978 Australian of the Year, negotiator of the Ranger mine agreement, for twenty-eight years chairman of the Northern Lands Council, and long-time Yirrkala Council member, with the use of a helicopter, four houses and a fleet of cars, has been called the Northern Territory's most powerful Aboriginal leader. According to Yunupingu, abuse of Aboriginal girls from Yirrkala, some as young as twelve, had been going on for fifteen years. A month earlier, Aboriginal elders in Boggabilla and Moree in New South Wales persuaded girls to speak to the media about their dealings with seasonal cotton workers and truckies who would accept 'nothing over sixteen'. One girl is supposed to have begun trading sexual favours with passing truckies at the age of eight. According to Judy Atkinson, Professor of Indigenous Studies at Southern Cross University, Aboriginal adolescents are abused in every state. Prostitution was unknown in pre-contact Aboriginal societies, but then so was suicide.

Prostitution is one extreme of the interaction between the white man and the black woman in Australia; the full spectrum includes all kinds of relationships, from the most casual to the most enduring, from coercive to collaborative. In 1929, Queensland's Protector of Aborigines, JW Bleakley, declared that 'a lubra is one of the greatest pioneers of the Territories, for without her it would have been impossible for the white man to have carried on'.[33] In other words, without the collusion and connivance of black women, white men could never have become established as the rulers and owners of the black homelands. Forty years later, the boss drover Matt Savage expressed the same opinion:

> It's no good saying one thing and meaning another: the outback would still have been in its wild state if it had not been for the lubras.[34]

Savage knew what he was talking about for he rode the stock routes of the inland for forty years; some of his best drover's boys were in fact Aboriginal women. In other circumstances, as in the Kimberley in the first decade of the twentieth century, when black men were rounded up and sent to jail, their womenfolk were coerced to give evidence against them, and then kept under police 'protection'.[35] By an array of similar strategies the white bosses contrived to drive a wedge between the Aboriginal man and the Aboriginal woman. As one Yolngu woman told the compilers of the *Little Children Are Sacred* report:

> Our communities are like a piece of broken string with women on one side and men on the other.[36]

According to anthropologists RM and CH Berndt, traditionally 'the most cherished possessions of men were women, children and their sacred heritage', in that order.[37] The European man who alienated the Aboriginal man's wife stole what was most important to him, and got away with it. The Aboriginal man's wife was not simply a woman he met by chance and fancied, but also his kinswoman, designated to be his wife from the time of her birth and possibly the only person he was eligible to marry. The dispossessed black man may have appeared to react with stoical resignation but it is the level of avoidance which signifies just how fundamental, how absolutely shattering this loss and humiliation must be. Discussion after discussion of the Aboriginal situation deals with every single outrage but the worst one. We know that the rape of an Aboriginal woman was a motivation for attacks on white settlements, which were then reported as instances of unmotivated savagery, but how often we cannot now say. The impression has been passed down that the black man allowed the white man to use his female kin with impunity, and indeed ignobly sought to exploit the relationship for his own benefit. This must surely exacerbate the black man's sense of humiliation and failure. Judy Atkinson puts it as delicately as she can:

> Aboriginal women and girls were sometimes able to make choices but most often they were driven by the need for food or protection from marauding white males, or violence had been the first persuader ... The myths that all Aboriginal women went willingly to the white intruders, or that the sexual trade

of Aboriginal women by Aboriginal men was normative on the frontier, must also be put aside. Sexual violence, as well as physical violence, was rampant on the frontier. What must also be named is that the experiences of colonisation were different for Aboriginal women in comparison to Aboriginal men. This created tension and disharmony in relationships between Aboriginal men and women that continues into the present.[38]

Atkinson describes herself as 'of Jiman and Bundjalung descent as well as having Celtic-German heritage'. Clearly Atkinson has no desire to libel her own forbears by insinuating that their relationships were abusive, but her way of putting the case is instructive. To say that not all Aboriginal women went willingly is to imply that some, perhaps even many, did; to say that something is not 'normative' is by no means to deny that it happened. Bertha Strehlow was so struck by the hardness of the life of the wife of a hunter she thought the decision to take up with a white man might at least sometimes have been prompted by the desire for a less arduous existence:

> it was the duty of the wife to fall behind her husband and carry all the household effects, the husband meanwhile walked ahead with no burdens to bear except a handful of spears ... In theory the man must be free to use his spears quickly when he sees game or catches sight of an enemy ... yet in practice this often means that the native woman has a very hard time. While her husband

walks along, swinging his arms freely, she is weighted down by heavy burdens and has to pause periodically to dig rabbits out of their burrows with her digging stick, collect grass seeds, and gather edible roots. At sun down when camp is made, it is the husband who has first taste of the food and first drink of water. If the supply is small, it is the wife who goes supperless to bed.[39]

If it is true that 'Aboriginal women were to be found wherever there was a white man's hut', it might also be the case that the black woman was making a choice in her own best interests and those of her children, but it should not be judged as a free choice. Often the community's sole chance of survival rested in their relationship through their womenfolk with the white invaders. In many cases it was a vain hope.

> The white man takes away his women and lives with them: but he does not fulfil any of the traditional obligations towards the native relatives of those women.[40]

The Aboriginal man had small choice but to follow his womenfolk into dependency upon the white man. Even if he still had access to drinkable water and there was still game to be hunted, without a woman he could not survive. Hunter-gatherer men are expendable but women are not, because hunters cannot survive without the contribution of gatherers. Hunting produces less, and less reliable, food supplies than gathering, which is the sole source of carbohydrate. A hunter-gather community in which men outnumber women to a significant extent faces starvation. If the white man couldn't survive in Australia without his 'lubra' the black man couldn't either. Where Aboriginal women went, humiliated Aboriginal men had no choice but to follow. As more and more Aboriginal men were deprived of reproductive opportunity, it was not long before traditional societies all over Australia began to exhibit a lack of children. Joshua Bray arrived in the Tweed Valley in 1862. Forty years later he wrote:

> black children are scarce now, I have not seen one for a year or more. In fact the blacks have almost died out.[41]

For Aboriginal men the agony of losing their womenfolk was not a simple matter of sexual jealousy. The marriage bond was an essential strand in the elastic network of kinship that constitutes Aboriginal society. It is not only the husband whose wife is abducted or runs away with another man who has a genuine cause of grievance. The whole community is affected and traditional justice may exact painful retribution from the guilty parties. When Jamie Gulpilil was asked to supply a scenario for Rolf de Heer's film *Ten Canoes*, he chose to tell a story that turns upon the abduction of a wife. Her husband has two other wives, but he is so outraged by the loss of his newest wife that he spears the man he thinks responsible, and kills the wrong man. As a punishment he is speared himself, and dies. A better allegory for the effect of wholesale wife-stealing by the white man can hardly be imagined. The husband's humiliation results in twofold destruction—of the innocent. The real culprits get off scot-free, as did the thousands of white men who laid waste the intricate web of kinship and mutual obligation that is Aboriginal society. For her part, the woman who opted for a white partner is unlikely to have done so in the expectation that he would dump her and his children back into the fractured Aboriginal community when he moved on. According to Noel Pearson, some 'mixed-blood children were in danger from their tribal stepfathers, while others were loved and treated as their own'.[42] Family resilience is a feature of hunter-gatherer families wherever they are found. No matter how tattered and torn the Aboriginal extended family, it cannot break.

Instead, it becomes the arena for the acting out of lethal rage.

The authorities both in Britain and in Australia were well aware of the whirlwind they would reap if the white man's inroads into black society could not be curtailed. One of the first acts of the Commonwealth when it took over administration of the Northern Territory from South Australia in 1911 was to institute the Office of Protector of Aborigines with the specific duty of limiting interracial intercourse. Protectors of Aborigines rode the ranges looking for white men with black women in their beds. Penalties were brought in for 'cohabitation'. The only result was that the black wives of white men and their children were sent to live in the blackfellas' camp rather than in the white man's house.

Then, though the children may have been fair-skinned, it was deemed that cohabitation could not be proved. The white man's children were called 'fatherless'. The very notion is an absurd evasion; there is no such thing as a fatherless child. When the white man walked away from his black family, no attempt was made to track him down for child support, even though his black relatives all knew who he was and the children probably all used his name. Instead, the state stepped in, in loco parentis, and gathered up the children he had discarded. Again and again in descriptions of the circumstances in which mixed-blood children were removed from an Aboriginal parent, that parent was a mother. We have no case where a part-Aboriginal child was forcibly removed from a white father, and not many where a part-Aboriginal child was removed from an Aboriginal father. In the vast majority of cases, the arms from which the children were torn were women's arms. Organisations like Fathers–4–Justice may rail against the common conception that the mother has first claim on a child, but historically fathers have only themselves to blame.

Sometimes it was the father himself who tore his children from their mother's arms and handed them over to an institution. Lowitja O'Donoghue made the painful discovery in the full glare of the public gaze that she was not taken from her mother by racist authorities, but sent to an institution by her white father, as were her five siblings by that same father. She cannot express rage towards him because he is her father but, by insisting on her Aboriginality in preference to her Irish heritage, in effect she disowns him, even though she keeps his name. Aboriginal communities are usually thought to have accepted pale-skinned children as full members, but if white society had rejected the children, or if the authorities treated them as Aboriginal, the community can hardly be said to have had a choice. A significant number of Australians have grown up oblivious of their Aboriginal inheritance, which in such cases must be entirely genetic, with no cultural component whatsoever, at least until such time as they make contact with their Aboriginal relatives. Since 1969, any person with any degree of Aboriginal ancestry who claimed to be Aboriginal and was accepted as such by an Aboriginal group, is identified as Aboriginal;

as a consequence the number and proportion of Aborigines in the Australian population has risen, as more and more Australians have discovered their Aboriginal roots. The traffic has been all one way. Stories of apparently white people discovering their Aboriginality abound, while there are no stories of Aboriginal people seeking out their white half-brothers and -sisters. The white person may choose to become Aboriginal, but, though the Aboriginal person may have three or four grandparents who are white, the converse is not equally true. It is as if white Australia will not accept anyone who is not of its colour while black Australia may not exclude anyone.

By 2010, according to demographer John Taylor, there will be 'one million Australians calling themselves Indigenous'. As Marcia

Langton pointed out in her Alfred Deakin lecture of 2001,

> there is a population explosion occurring in the Aboriginal and Torres Strait Islander populations. Whereas, presently, most Australians are able to dismiss Aboriginal demands for justice as the complaints of a miniscule minority, their children will not be able to so avoid the problem. Indeed, the injustice and inequity will exponentially increase for indigenous people as ordinary citizenship entitlements, such as education and health care, fail to keep up with a rapidly increasing population. Even on the most conservative figures, the Indigenous population is currently expanding at a rate more than twice that of the total population,

with an average annual rate of growth of around 2.3 per cent.

The leap in the numbers of the Aboriginal and Islander populations between 1991 and 1996 has been explained as a consequence of two factors, one being the increase in the numbers of people self-identifying as Aboriginal and the other 'that many children of Indigenous origin have one rather than two parents of Indigenous origin'.[43] Fewer than half of the self-identified Aboriginal and Torres Strait Islander families are likely to be headed by an Aboriginal or Islander male. According to the 1996 census, Aboriginal women were almost as likely to be married to or cohabiting with a non-Aboriginal man as with an Aboriginal man.[44] The trend has been established for more than thirty years; of eighty-two family units sampled for a study of poverty in Aboriginal families in Adelaide in 1975, only twenty-six were headed by Aboriginal men, the rest being headed by Aboriginal women or white men.[45] What David McKnight observed on Mornington Island, that 'many young women favoured Whites because they treated them better',[46] can be witnessed all over Australia. A man who is accident-prone and permanently in trouble disqualifies himself from playing the father role; as his ceremonial role has withered away, and there is no more hunting to be done, he becomes more and more of a burden on the indigenous community. The fact that government welfare payments are often made to women, for the very good reason that they are more likely to be spent on family needs than tobacco, alcohol and gambling, means that more and more women can live independently of men, and are doing so.

> The Aboriginal family norm is increasingly matrifocal, leaving more boys and youths in single-parent, female-headed families deprived of male role models. This trend is evident in the wider population, but is much more acute among black families. In its most extreme form it involves indigenous grandmothers being left to raise and support many grandchildren on a single pension.[47]

When hunter-gatherer societies begin to break down, it is invariably the gatherers, the women, who combine to hold them together, but in doing so they further marginalise their menfolk, including their own sons.

> That women are overwhelmingly taking on such responsibilities [fighting the grog runners and running night patrols] tells us much about the emasculation of indigenous male identity. Understanding this is central to understanding the dynamics of black family violence. Without this understanding it is too easy to resort to racist stereotypes suggesting that indigenous men are inherently violent or alcoholic, or that rape and assault of women went unpunished in traditional society.[48]

Rosemary Neill's observation suggests a corollary. As men find themselves less and less able to function as family heads, and less and less welcome as members of the household, we might expect their rage and destructiveness to escalate. Domestic violence has brought about the distancing of women and children from adult men, and distancing provokes more violence. The rejected male becomes a marauder in his own community. Some anthropologists have suggested that violence was the way that the hunter-gatherer male traditionally enforced his authority over his wife. The truth seems to be rather that when the Aboriginal husband lost cultural authority over his wife his only resort was violence. Even so, pervasive domestic violence in Aboriginal households is by no means new. When I was first in Alice Springs, in 1972, I was shocked to see how many women were carrying injuries, some of them quite serious. I was told that they had been bashed for 'being cheeky'; what this meant was that they had referred to forbidden matters when they were drunk, something that would have happened very rarely in traditional society, if ever. Observance of such taboos was practically the only remnant of ritual culture the men had left. The women wanted me to understand that by transgressing they had 'asked for it', but the punishment, the 'good hiding', involving fists, sticks and bottles, seemed crazily excessive. What I witnessed then was the operation of rage; in the thirty-six years since it has only got worse. According to Colin Tatz, suicide was unknown in Aboriginal communities until thirty years ago; Aboriginal communities now exhibit one of the highest suicide rates in the world.[49]

A caged animal will reject its young and even kill them. A man prevented from defending his rights and dignity may attack his wife, his children and himself. Most people think that people commit suicide because they are very sad; suicide is more often an act of terminal rage. The rape and murder of one's own children is an elaboration of this profound aggression towards oneself. The process begins very early when Aboriginal children defy their parents and chase oblivion by sniffing glue or petrol. It goes on when they start driving, in unsafe vehicles, on roads that never see a grader, much too fast for the conditions, deliberately risking life and limb. Their Aboriginal great-grandparents could express themselves forcefully and accurately in several languages; today's children can neither speak nor write a single language. Often homeless, jobless, illiterate, with neither driver's licence, birth certificate nor Medicare card, the young Aboriginal male has virtually no chance of staying on the right side of the law. Lawless behaviour is the nearest he can come to resistance.

In 1999, a taskforce of fifty Aboriginal and Torres Strait Islander women produced a report on domestic violence for the Queensland government, thereby breaking the rule that such matters were not to be discussed before outsiders. The atrocities they brought to light were horrifying. In view of the prediction that Aboriginal and Torres Strait Islander Australians would number a million by 2010, the women's conclusion that 'increasing injuries and fatalities as a result of interpersonal violence ... threaten the continued existence of Australia's indigenous peoples' seems contradictory.[50] The reported levels of rape alone were so high that they would have sufficed to render the communities non-viable. Of seventy-six homicides in Queensland in the five years from 1993 to 1998, more than a third of victims and almost 50 per cent of perpetrators were drawn from the 2.4 per cent of the state's population that is Aboriginal or Torres Strait Islander. At the same time Audrey Bolger found that, taking both reported and unreported instances of assault into account, almost one in three Aboriginal women living in the Northern Territory could expect to be assaulted in the course of a year. More Aboriginal women would die as a consequence of domestic violence than inmates would die in custody.[51]

For the readers of *Witchetty's Tribe*, subtitled *Aboriginal Cartoon Fun*, Eric Jolliffe's comic periodical of the 1940s and 1950s, featuring as it did sub-pornographic images of curvaceous black females covered with bruises and bandages, and black men with clubs, Aboriginal domestic violence was a joke. In reality it is anything but.

Women who have been repeatedly beaten deteriorate over the years. Medically speaking they die of kidney failure, heart attack, liver complaint, and the like. But their deaths have really been caused or hastened by physical ill-treatment. At least three women [on Mornington Island] have been so badly beaten that they have suffered brain damage and are unable to walk or talk properly ... Women in particular have suffered facial disfigurement from kicks, punches, blows from sticks and cuts from knives. Many young women have broken noses and jaws so that their faces are asymmetrical. The flesh on their face, particularly lips and nose, is permanently swollen with the result that their features are ruined.[52]

All kinds of causes are adduced for the escalating violence in indigenous communities; what is remarkable is that it is all expressed within those communities. The black man does not turn his rage on his enemy but upon his friend, and therefore on himself.

By attacking his womenfolk and his children, the black man is writing himself out of their history. The new Aboriginals of the year 2010 will not include him. Because of the mayhem that is ripping Aboriginal communities apart Prime Minister Howard could rely on popular support for the Northern Territory Intervention, by which all the gains that had been made for indigenous Australians in the Territory were cancelled. Self-determination had failed; indigenous communities were once more to be administered directly from Canberra. The prime minister had responded to the call of the women to come to the aid of them and their children. Once more the white man was being chosen over the dysfunctional black man as the protector of children. The defeat of the black man was absolute.

When Marcia Langton, who as an activist had worked so hard for so long and so effectively for land rights, declared her support for the Northern Territory Intervention in November 2007, she emphasised the extent to which it was a victory of right-minded women over wrong-headed men:

> The combined effect of the media campaign for action and the emergency intervention has been a metaphorical dagger sunk into the heart of the powerful, wrong-headed Aboriginal male ideology that had prevailed in indigenous affairs, policies and practices.[53]

The apology for the stolen generations has been called a 'divisive farce' because so many white Australians believed they had nothing to apologise for. What we have witnessed in the case of the Intervention may have caused division not only between white blindfold and black armband but also between black women and black men. Langton here seems to be insisting on the needs of women and children as life-and-death matters taking precedence over politics but, if I am right in believing that rage is the driver of dysfunction in indigenous communities, the Intervention will do nothing to assuage it and may indeed make matters worse. The already persecuted women will be seen as having colluded with the enemy to remove the few strands of self-esteem the indigenous man had left. Two of the women involved in preparing the Women's Task Force on Violence report were obliged to withdraw from the project before it was completed, after they were physically attacked in their own communities.

Our notions of the role of violence in Aboriginal domestic relations are confused. Historically, women were warned away from men's secret rituals by histrionic threats of gang rape. American anthropologist VK Burbank argues that Aborigines accept physical aggression as a 'legitimate form of social action' and limit it through ritual and that women know how to deal with physical aggression, unlike their western counterparts.[54] D Bell, on the other hand, argues that violence towards Kaytej women increased with 'settlement life', largely as a consequence of alcohol abuse.[55] Robert Tonkinson summarises the current state of our understanding thus:

> The evidence with respect to gender role transformations in Aboriginal Australia

in the wake of European invasion is both sparse and conflicting. Departing mainly from conclusions reached via their reconstructions of the traditional situation some writers have argued for a diminution in women's autonomy and greater oppression than was believed to be the case prior to European settlement, others for an increase in women's status and power vis-a-vis men and still others remain equivocal in their assessment of the situation. All such conclusions could of course be right since they pertain to different areas and different points in time, but much depends on the view these scholars take of the pre-colonial situation.[56]

In fact there was great diversity in the status and treatment of women across the whole spectrum of Aboriginal society. What is now undeniable is that violence towards women and children across the same spectrum has reached the level of race suicide.

The Aboriginal women who have begged for state protection have no other recourse, but that protection is unlikely to be effective if the problem of rage is not confronted. The problem we have with the agonising rage of hunter-gatherers is that we can't just tell them to get over it. It's all they have. There will be those who accept reconciliation, who will make the best of a bad job, most of them women. Then there are those who would rather die. Who will have none of it. Who do not want a whitefella house, whitefella handout, whitefella bullshit. Government ministers who have flown into town and told them to clean up their graffiti, control their dogs and send their kids to school have been sent about their business in the rudest terms. The choice to go bush is made in desperation, as if it were the declaration of an intention to die with country. And country is dying. Katter was wrong in his figures; the land now under prickly acacia amounts to 6.6 million hectares. Prickly acacia is just one of the weeds that has reduced the biodiversity of the inland until there is nothing left to hunt. Graziers like buffel grass but it is spinifex that supports the species that provide the hunter-gatherer diet. Spinifex is losing to buffel grass, which is spreading exponentially, like smoke. When fire comes through, buffel grass burns too long, heating the subsoil and killing the roots of the river red gums that are the glory of the inland.

Everywhere in Australia bush tucker has become harder and harder to find; the valiant women who take their children bush have to resist their constant whingeing for hamburgers and Coke. Kids living on outstations want the same things as kids in the suburbs. Life on the outstations is dangerous: the roads are seldom if ever graded; there is no teacher in the school, no doctor in the clinic, no wholesome food in the store. Living dispersed puts demands on the infrastructure that no Australian government has ever been prepared to underwrite; outstations are reviled as living museums. We'll see if the Rudd Labor government has a better understanding of what it means to put your money where your mouth is. There's not much point in building houses for Aboriginal people if there is no decent road, and therefore no fresh vegetables or fruit and only rotisserie chicken and frozen mutton chops in the store. Meanwhile, more Aboriginal children are still being taken into care. A new generation is being stolen—sorry—removed. If the dieback of Aboriginal communities is to be reversed, the rage that is destroying blackfellas must be recognised and managed. Denial has taken us to annihilating excesses of insanity and self-destructive behaviour that are resented as if they were inexplicable, when the causes are obvious.

Rage is toxic; untreated rage can be lethal. Even low levels of rage can shorten your life. A recent article in the *New England Journal of Medicine* argues that driving is bad for our health, not primarily because of pollutants in the atmosphere but because of the stress and anger that drivers suffer. If simply sitting in traffic increases the risk of heart attack threefold, we cannot be surprised if the Aboriginal man's heart fails him at fifty. 'Anger turned inward may cause hypertension, high blood pressure or depression.'[57] Australian Aboriginal people suffer high levels of all three. The antidote to poisoning by rage is assertion; assertion requires a forum and a recognised status within that forum. All over the world, except in Australia, hunter-gatherer peoples have organised resistance, resistance to destruction of country, to inappropriate exploitation, to loss of privacy and autonomy, to corruption of culture. As minorities, sometimes tiny minorities, their resistance is unlikely ultimately to hold back the processes of colonisation, and even in Canada, as the example of the Ojibwa shows, the outrages and the misery proliferate. Nevertheless in Africa, Asia and the Americas, hunter-gatherer peoples have access to ways of asserting themselves that are not available to the first Australians. All of them, except the Australians, have a treaty and can exert themselves to enforce its observance. In not arriving at a treaty we leave Aboriginal people prey to the worst kind of rage, the helpless kind.

People now talk of establishing an annual sorry day, as if it would do Whitey good to remind himself how magnanimous he was on 13 February 2008. More useful would be an annual angry day, when Whitey would get reminded of just what he has done for Australia. It was not the blackfella who killed the Murray-Darling river system, who ripped the guts out of the Pilbara, who poisoned

Woomera, who introduced cinnamon fungus, who silted up the rivers of the east coast, who logged, felled and burned the rainforest, who is now destroying Port Phillip Bay and squandering the water of the artesian basin. Australians are now becoming aware of the dire plight of their island continent, and the utter bleakness of its future. If they are to master the discipline that enabled hunter-gatherer peoples to live off that same land for 60 000 years, they need to learn a new set of priorities and a new way of life. We need a hunter-gatherer presence in Australian politics every bit as much as the black man needs a political structure that will enable him to focus and direct his rage towards something other than himself and his people.

Notes

1 Hansard, 13 February 2008, p. 261.
2 *Ibid.*, pp. 258–9.
3 *Ibid.*, p. 262.
4 *Ibid.*
5 Hansard, 13 June 2007, p. 31.
6 Hansard, 16 March 2005, p. 36.
7 Hansard, 13 February 2008, p. 261.
8 As reported in *The Australian*, 12 February 2008.
9 Australian Bureau of Statistics, *Prisoners in Australia 2004* (ABS catalogue no. 4501.0), Canberra, 2004.
10 *Ibid.*; see also Australian Institute of Criminology, *Australian Crime Facts and Figures 2005*, Australian Institute of Criminology, Canberra, 2006.

NOTES

11 *Ibid.*

12 *Queensland Corrections*, 1999; see also Ian O'Connor, 'The New Removals: Aboriginal Youth in the Queensland Juvenile Justice System', *International Social Work*, 37, 1994, pp. 197–212.

13 Vickie Dalton, Melanie Brown and David McDonald, *Australian Deaths in Custody & Custody-Related Police Operations, 1995*, Australian Institute of Criminology, Canberra, 1996.

14 Jacqueline Joudo and Marissa Veld, *Deaths in Custody in Australia: National Deaths in Custody Annual Report 2004*, Australian Institute of Criminology, Canberra, 2005.

15 Megan Lewis, *Weekend Australian*, 29–30 March 2008.

16 Judy Atkinson, *Trauma Trails, Recreating Song Lines: The Transgenerational Effects of Trauma in Indigenous Australia*, Spinifex Press, Melbourne, 2002, pp. 54–5.

17 Christopher Vecsey, *Traditional Ojibwa Religion and its Historic Changes*, Social Science Books,

Toronto, 1983, pp. 199–200; Marci McDonald, 'Horrors of Minimata Haunt Canadian Indians', *Audubon 78*, no. 2, pp. 125–9; Joseph McLeod, *And the Rivers Our Blood*, Social Science Books, Toronto, 1977; Warner Troyer, *No Safe Place*, Social Science Books, Toronto, 1977.

18 L Hiatt, HC Coombs and BC Dexter, 'The Outstation Movement in Aboriginal Australia', in E Leacock and R Lee (eds), *Politics and History: Band Societies*, Cambridge University Press, Cambridge, 1982.

19 Anastasia M Shkilnyk, *A Poison Greater than Love*, Yale University Press, New Haven, 1985, p. 11.

20 Rosemary Neill, *White Out: How Politics is Killing Black Australia*, Allen & Unwin, Sydney, 2002, p. 133.

21 Gillian Cowlishaw, *Black, White or Brindle: Race in Rural Australia*, Cambridge University Press, Cambridge, 1988, p. 3.

22 Dailapi, quoted in T Petrie, *Reminiscences of Early Queensland*, Watson and Ferguson, Brisbane, 1904, pp. 182–3.

23 Richard Broome, *Aboriginal Australians: Black Responses to White Dominance 1788–2001*, Allen & Unwin, Sydney, 2002, third edition, p. 59; *cf.* A Hamilton, 'Blacks and Whites: The Relationships of Change', *Arena*, 30, 1972, p. 42.

24 R Tonkinson, 'Gender Transformation among Australian Aborigines', in Peter P Schweitzer, Megan Biesele and Robert K Hitchcock (eds), *Hunters and Gatherers in the Modern World: Conflict, Resistance and Self-Determination*, Berghahn Books, New York and Oxford, 2000, p. 353; *cf.* Tonkinson, 'The Changing Status of Aboriginal Women: Free Agents at Jigalong', in *Going it Alone: Prospects for Aboriginal Autonomy*, Aboriginal Studies Press, Canberra, 1990.

25 *Hedland Advocate*, 25 January 1908, quoted in Mary Anne Jebb, *Blood, Sweat and Welfare: A History of White Bosses and Black Pastoral Workers*, University of Western Australia Press, Perth, 2002, p. 64.

26 Frank Clune, *Roaming around the Darling*, Angus & Robertson, Sydney, 1952, p. 82; Bruce Elder, *Blood on the Wattle: Massacres and Maltreatment*

of *Aboriginal Australians Since 1788*, New Holland Publishers, Sydney, 2003, pp. 134–5, 221, 228; Jebb, *Blood, Sweat and Welfare*, pp. 129–30, 297; M Jackson, *At Home in the World*, Harper Perennial, Sydney, 1995, pp. 95-6.

27 Elder, *Blood on the Wattle*, p. 34.
28 R Evans, K Saunders and K Cronin, *Exclusion, Exploitation and Extermination: Race Relations in Colonial Queensland*, Australian and New Zealand Book Company, Sydney, 1975, p. 107; Ann McGrath, *Born in the Cattle: Aborigines in Cattle Country*, Allen & Unwin, Sydney, 1987.
29 Ward McNally, *Aborigines, Artefacts and Anguish*, Lutheran Publishing House, Adelaide, 1981, p. 82.
30 *Aboriginal Women Speak Out — about Rape and Child Sexual Abuse: A Report of an Adelaide Survey, October 1985 – May 1986, Conducted in the Aboriginal Community*, Adelaide Rape Crisis Centre Inc., Adelaide, 1987 (i.e., 42 per cent as compared to 41 per cent; 17 per cent were pack rapes).

NOTES

31 Queensland State Archives, 7328/271644, 271655, WE Roth, Protector of Aborigines, Reports to the Commissioner of Police, 1898.
32 *The Australian*, 4 April 2008.
33 JW Bleakley, *The Aboriginals and Half-Castes of Central Australia and North Australia*, Commonwealth Government Printer, Canberra, 1929, p. 7.
34 Keith Willey, *Boss Drover*, Rigby, Adelaide, 1971, p. 18.
35 Jebb, *Blood, Sweat and Welfare*, pp. 40–4.
36 *Ampe Akelyernemane Meke Mekarle 'Little Children are Sacred'*: Report of the Northern Territory Board of Enquiry into the Protection of Aboriginal Children from Sexual Abuse, p. 59.
37 RM and CH Berndt, *The World of the First Australians*, Aboriginal Studies Press, Canberra, 1985, p. 225.
38 Atkinson, *Trauma Trails*, pp. 62–3.
39 Bertha Strehlow, 'Glimpses of Lubra Life in Central Australia', AFA Annual Report, 1949, p. 34.

NOTES

40　TGH Strehlow, 'Notes on Native Evidence and its value', *Oceania* VI, no. 3, March 1936, p. 331.

41　Joshua Bray, 'Tribal Districts and Customs', *Science of Man*, 4 (1), 1901, pp. 9–10.

42　Noel Pearson, *The Australian*, 12 February 2008.

43　Australian Bureau of Statistics, *Occasional Paper: Population Issues, Indigenous Australians*, 1997, 9; cf. *Population Distribution, Aboriginal and Torres Strait Islander Australians*, 2006.

44　1996 census, Australian Bureau of Statistics, Canberra, 1998.

45　Fay Gale and Joan Binnion, *Poverty among Aboriginal Families in Adelaide*, Australian Government Commission of Enquiry into Poverty, Australian Government Publishing Service, Canberra, 1975.

46　David McKnight, *From Hunting to Drinking: The Devastating Effects of Alcohol on an Australian Aboriginal Community*, Routledge, London and New York, 2002, p. 98.

47　Neill, *White Out*, p. 101.

48　*Ibid.*, p. 100.

49 Colin Tatz, *Aboriginal Suicide is Different: A Portrait of Life and Self-Destruction*, Aboriginal Studies Press, Canberra, 2001, p. 25.

50 *Report of Aboriginal and Torres Strait Islander Women's Task Force on Violence*, State of Queensland, 1999, quoting Australian Aboriginal Affairs Council, briefing document, Darwin, 1990.

51 Audrey Bolger, *Aboriginal Women and Violence*, for the Criminology Research Council and Northern Territory Commissioner of Police, Darwin, North Australia Research Unit, Australian National University, Canberra, 1991.

52 McKnight, *From Hunting to Drinking*, p. 121.

53 Marcia Langton, 'It's Time to Stop Playing Politics with Vulnerable Lives', 30 November 2007, viewed at http://culture matters. wordpress.com/2007/11/30/marcia-langton-on-the-nt-intervention; *cf.* Gale and Binnion, *Poverty among Aboriginal Families in Adelaide*, *passim*.

54 VK Burbank, *Fighting Women: Anger and Aggression in Aboriginal Australia*, University of California Press, Berkeley, 1994, *passim*.

NOTES

55 D Bell, *Daughters of the Dreaming*, McPhee Gribble, Melbourne, 1984.
56 Tonkinson, 'Gender Transformation among Australian Aborigines', p. 353.
57 A Peters *et al.*, 'Exposure to Traffic and the Onset of Myocardial Infarction', *New England Journal of Medicine*, 21 October 2004, 351:17, pp. 1721–30.